QUAKER QUOTES

GW00538028

William Sessions Limited
York, England

ISBN 978-1-85072-369-1

We delayed publication of *Quaker Quotes*
for six months while, with the help
of Heather Rowland, former Librarian of the Library
of the Religious Society of Friends in Britain,
we tried to contact all individual copyright holders
of quotations published in *Quaker Faith and Practice*.
We apologise to any whose addresses we have
been unable to find and we wish to thank
Heather Rowland for her efforts on our behalf.
All royalties will go to the Bursary Fund,
which will help more young people to attend
Saffron Walden Friends School.

Printed in Palatino Typeface
from Author's Disk
by Sessions of York
The Ebor Press
York, England

Quaker Faith and Practice is an astonishing book, a tremendous overflowing cornucopia of wisdom and beauty – so overflowing that it is difficult to pick up and consult as often as one would wish to.

Kahlil Gibran's *The Prophet*
stays in our sitting rooms year
after year and is consulted often –
another book full of wisdom
and beauty.

Out of deep admiration for both
these books we have collected wise
and arresting thoughts of
Quakers through the centuries,
speaking out about what they
have found to be true.
We have tried to make a small book
to stay in the living room and be
picked up and consulted often.

Included in this collection are
quotes from *Advices & Queries,*
the little red book kept for use on
the central table of Quaker
Meetings across the world.

Table of Contents

The full titles of the book and booklet
familiar to Quakers across the world are:

Quaker Faith & Practice: the book of
Christian discipline of the
Yearly Meeting of the Religious Society
of Friends (Quakers) in Britain.
– 3rd ed. 2005. Published by
Britain Yearly Meeting.

and

Advices and Queries: the Yearly
Meeting of the Religious Society of
Friends (Quakers) in Britain.
– 3rd ed. 2005. Published by
Britain Yearly Meeting.

1. WE ARE THE CHILDREN OF THE LIGHT

Sing and rejoice, ye Children of the Day and of the Light; for the Lord is at work in this thick night of Darkness that may be felt; and Truth doth flourish as the rose, and the lilies do grow among the thorns, and the plants atop of the hills, and upon them the lambs doth skip and play. And never heed the tempests nor the storms, floods nor rains, for the Seed Christ is over all and doth reign. And so, be of good faith and valiant for the Truth.

George Fox, 1663
Faith and Practice (20.23)

 ake heed, dear friends, to the promptings of love and truth in your hearts. Trust them as the leadings of God whose Light shows us our darkness and brings us to new life.

Advices & Queries, 1

In this humanistic age we suppose man is the initiator and God is the responder. But the living Christ within us is the initiator and we are the responders. God the Lover, the accuser, the revealer of light and darkness presses within us.

'Behold, I stand at the door and knock.'

And all our apparent initiative is already a response, a testimonial to His secret pressure and working within us. The basic response of the soul to the Light is internal adoration and joy, thanksgiving and worship, self-surrender and listening.

Thomas R Kelly, 1941
Faith and Practice (2.10)

Do not look for such great matters to begin
with; but be content to be a child and let the
Father proportion out daily to thee what light,
what power, what exercises, what straits, what
fears, what troubles he sees fit for thee; and do
thou bow before him continually in humility of
heart. Thou must join in with the beginnings of
life, and be exercised with the day of small
things, before thou meet with the great things…
The rest is at noonday; but the travels begin
at the breaking of day, wherein are but
glimmerings or little light, wherein the
discovery of good and evil are not so manifest
and certain; yet there must the traveller begin
and in his faithful travels the light will break
in upon him more and more.

Isaac Penington, 1665
Faith and Practice (19.43)

O! ye young men and women ... look to the rock of your fathers; there is no other God but him, no other Light but his, no other grace but his, nor spirit but his, to convince you, quicken you, comfort you; to lead, guide and preserve you to God's everlasting kingdom. So will you be possessors as well as professors of the truth, embracing it not only by education but judgment and conviction; from a sense begotten in your souls, through the operation of the eternal spirit and power of God in your hearts.

William Penn, 1693
Faith and Practice (19.59)

2. WE MUST TRY TO LIVE LOVINGLY

What matters is living our lives in the power of love... Hence we lose the sense of helplessness and futility in the face of the world's crushing problems... We must literally not take too much thought for the morrow but throw ourselves wholeheartedly into the present.
That is the beauty of the way of love; it cannot be planned and its end cannot be foretold.

Wolf Mendl, 1974
Faith and Practice (24.60)

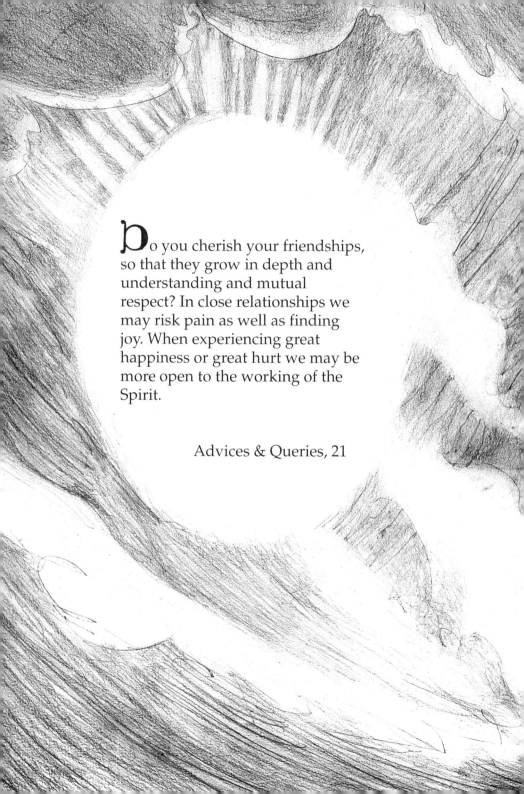

Do you cherish your friendships, so that they grow in depth and understanding and mutual respect? In close relationships we may risk pain as well as finding joy. When experiencing great happiness or great hurt we may be more open to the working of the Spirit.

Advices & Queries, 21

Love is the hardest lesson in Christianity; but for that reason it should be most our care to learn it.

William Penn, 1643
Faith and Practice (22.01)

I can think with thankfulness of friends who have brought light to my darkness – perhaps a single sentence, a friendly letter, a walk on the downs: The help was perhaps given unconsciously but it was because they were sensitive to God's leadings that they were able to do it. Do we seek to be the channels of God's love and caring?
'Caring matters most'. (Friedrich von Hügel)

Edward H Milligan, 1951
Faith and Practice (21.20)

I have found in my life that from time to time when revelling in new-found joys or faced with decision, problem or grief, there must be for me a listening ear. Even if my listener says little but sheds over me a feeling of rejoicing with me, of being alongside me as I strive or sorrowing with me in my hour of distress, then I can better appreciate or face the situation. I believe this is true for most of us. There are moments when we need one another. If this sometimes unuttered cry is answered, then truly we meet, and do not grope or slip past each other. But if two individuals share at an even deeper level from their own experience in their search for ultimate reality in life, then the divine in the human shines through and a new creation is born for both.

Margaret Gibbins, 1969
Faith and Practice (21.15)

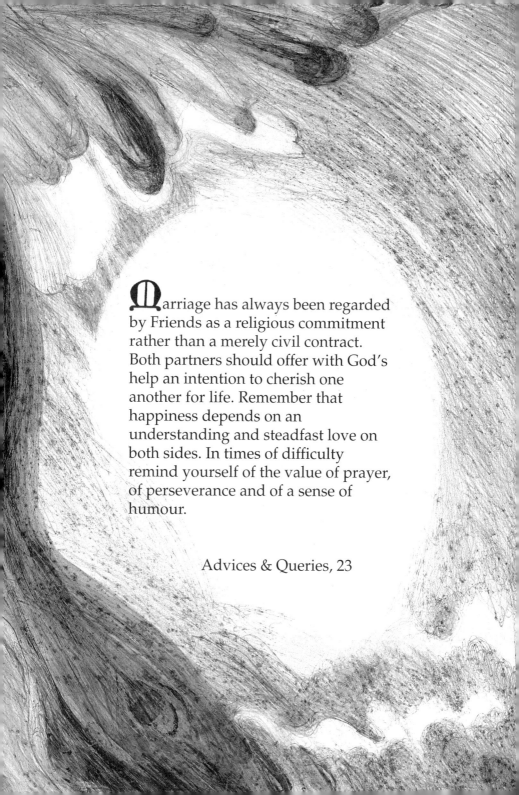

Marriage has always been regarded by Friends as a religious commitment rather than a merely civil contract. Both partners should offer with God's help an intention to cherish one another for life. Remember that happiness depends on an understanding and steadfast love on both sides. In times of difficulty remind yourself of the value of prayer, of perseverance and of a sense of humour.

Advices & Queries, 23

$\mathbf{I}$ think parents need to be aware of how vital it is to leave everything to answer a young child's reaching out to you to 'come quickly' to share a sunset or the beauty of a discovered wild flower, or the trick of the pet dog, or to listen with full attention, no matter what seems prior on your agenda, when children burst into the house from school eager to have you listen to a tale of woe or a triumph they have experienced during the day. There is little question that if as a parent we have not taken the time really to listen to children when they are young, listened not only to their words but to their feelings behind the words, they are unlikely to want to come with their sharings in later life. Learning to listen to each other in families can help to make us better listeners to others and to the Inner Guide.

Dorothy Steere, 1984
Faith and Practice (22.62)

Do you recognise the needs and gifts of each member of your family and household, not forgetting your own? Try to make your home a place of loving friendship and enjoyment, where all who live or visit may find the peace and refreshment of God's presence.

Advices & Queries, 26

How do we become reconciled to each other if we are asunder? All I can say is to go up to that person and say what is in your heart; that their ways are hurting but you still love them. But this takes time and not many people like to look in a person's face and find out who they are. So we miss the reconciliation and do not have the experience that we *cared*. Given that, then we will know who we are and find relief in tears we all should share. This is where peace starts.

Sue Norris, 1982
Faith and Practice (20.68)

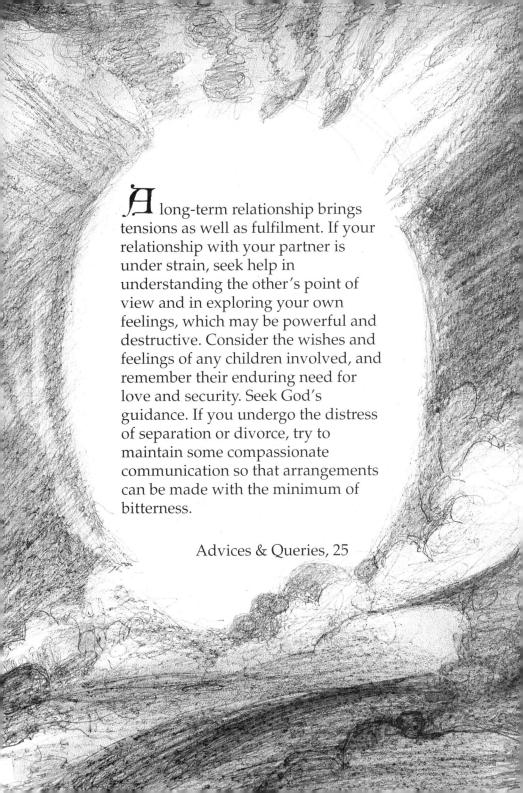

A long-term relationship brings tensions as well as fulfilment. If your relationship with your partner is under strain, seek help in understanding the other's point of view and in exploring your own feelings, which may be powerful and destructive. Consider the wishes and feelings of any children involved, and remember their enduring need for love and security. Seek God's guidance. If you undergo the distress of separation or divorce, try to maintain some compassionate communication so that arrangements can be made with the minimum of bitterness.

Advices & Queries, 25

ħave you ever sat with a friend when in the course of an easy and pleasant conversation the talk took a new turn and you both listened avidly to one another and to something that was emerging in your visit? You found yourselves saying things that astonished you and finally you stopped talking and there was an immense naturalness about the long silent pause that followed. In that silent interval you were possessed by what you had discovered together. If this has happened to you, you know that when you come up out of such an experience, there is a memory of rapture and a feeling in the heart of having touched holy ground.

Douglas Steere, 1955
Faith and Practice (22.09)

3. LET US PRAY ...

Dear Lord and Father of mankind
Forgive our foolish ways!
Reclothe us in our rightful mind,
In purer lives thy service find,
In deeper reverence, praise.

Drop thy still dews of quietness,
Till all our strivings cease;
Take from our souls the strain and stress,
And let our ordered lives confess
The beauty of thy peace.

Breathe through the heats of our desire
Thy coolness and thy balm;
Let sense be dumb, let flesh retire;
Speak through the earthquake, wind and fire,
O still small voice of calm!

John Greenleaf Whittier, 1892
Faith and Practice (20.03)

Worship is essentially an act of adoration, adoration of the one true God in whom we live and move and have our being.

Forgetting our little selves, our petty ambitions, our puny triumphs, our foolish cares and fretful anxieties, we reach out towards the beauty and majesty of God.

The religious life is not a dull, grim drive towards moral virtues, but a response to a vision of greatness.

Thomas F Green, 1952
Faith and Practice (2.07)

Begin now, as you read these words, as you sit in your chair, to offer your whole selves, utterly and in joyful abandon, in quiet, glad surrender to Him who is within. In secret ejaculation of praise, turn in humble wonder to the Light, faint though it may be.

Keep contact with the outer world of sense and meanings. Here is no discipline in absent-mindedness. Walk and talk and work and laugh with your friends. But behind the scenes keep up the life of simple prayer and inward worship. Keep it up throughout the day. Let inward prayer be your last act before you fall asleep and the first act when you awake. And in time you will find, as did Brother Lawrence, that 'those who have the gale of the Holy Spirit go forward even in sleep'.

Thomas R Kelly, 1941
Faith and Practice (2.22)

Prayer is an exercise of the spirit, as thought is of the mind. To pray about anything is to use the powers of our spirit on it, just as to think clearly is to use our mental powers. For the best solution of every problem, the best carrying out of every action, both thought and prayer are necessary... To pray about any day's work does not mean to ask success in it. It means, first to realise my own inability to do even a familiar job as it truly should be done, unless I am in touch with eternity, unless I do it 'unto God'. It means to see 'my' work as part of a whole, to see 'myself' as not mattering much, but my faith, the energy, will and striving which I put into the work as mattering a great deal.

Mary F Smith, 1936
Faith and Practice (20.08)

I ask for daily bread, but not for wealth, lest I
   forget the poor.
I ask for strength, but not for power, lest I
   despise the meek.
I ask for wisdom, but not for learning, lest I
   scorn the simple.
I ask for a clean name, but not for fame, lest I
   contemn the lowly.
I ask for peace of mind, but not for idle hours,
   lest I fail to hearken to the call of duty.

Inazo Nitobe, 1909
Faith and Practice (20.01)

4. WE MUST TRY TO BE MORE LIKE JESUS

I cannot explain the mystery of how someone who is a human being just as I am can also be worshipped. And yet the more real the mystery has become for me, it isn't that Jesus has become more like God, but that all my brothers and sisters have. It is through him that I recognise God in my neighbour – through Jesus I've discovered the uniqueness of everyone. And there was in him a quality of willingness to be defeated and destroyed by his enemies and to go on loving them, that alone made possible a new quality of life afterwards.

Paul Oestreicher, 1981
Faith and Practice (26.53)

I decided long ago that God was not the most 'powerful' thing in the universe. He much more resembles a barefoot Galilean prophet speaking in up-country dialect, followed by tax-gatherers, fishermen and prostitutes, who becomes a nuisance and ends up (very properly) by being crucified while the guards dice for his clothes – more to pass the time than because the garments are worth anything. It is not because God is powerful that I worship him; if he is powerful it is in some dimension that I don't know anything about, which we can agree (if you like) to call eternity… No, the moment when I love God is at the moment when the Galilean prophet was watching his followers melt away and suspected that Simon Peter the fisherman would soon be off too, back to his nets.

'Wilt thou also go away?' he asks Simon; but mercifully Simon is too stupid to see the point of the question, or to take his chance to get out. 'Lord, to whom should we go? Thou hast the word of eternal life.'

That's it, the obscure, futile, shaky thing as feeble as a baby in a stable, that's what I worship.

J Ormerod Greenwood, 1973
Faith and Practice (26.57)

In this day and age the place where Friends find their unity is in the kind of God they worship. Their apprehension of the relationship of Jesus Christ to God embraces every orthodox and unorthodox shade of theology from Unitarian to Trinitarian, but whether we regard Jesus … as God himself or as the supreme revealer of God to man, it is the same kind of God: a spirit of peace, truth, love and redeeming power. We need to feel the influence of this Spirit in our lives rather than to argue about our different modes of apprehending him… Let us keep our different modes of apprehension and remember always that it is the same God we serve, revealing himself to each according to his faith, his openness and his needs.

Beatrice Saxon Snell, 1960
Faith and Practice (26.77)

The Religious Society of Friends is rooted in Christianity and has always found inspiration in the life and teachings of Jesus. How do you interpret your faith in the light of this heritage? How does Jesus speak to you today? Are you following Jesus' example of love in action?

Advices & Queries, 4

We know that Jesus identified himself with the suffering and the sinful, the poor and the oppressed… We know that he warned us against the deceitfulness of riches, that wealth and great possessions so easily come between us and God, and divide us from our neighbours. He respected the common folk… and was more hopeful of a response from them than from the well-to-do, the clever and the learned. Yet he never fostered in them feelings of envy and hatred. He called them to love their enemies and pray for them that despitefully used them. He makes us all ashamed that we are not all out in caring for our fellow men.

H G Wood, 1958
Faith and Practice (23.03)

'I and the Father are One'. That means to me that I think of God in terms of Jesus Christ, that I pray to Jesus as representing the Father or to the Father as I see him in Jesus. Carry the thought to Calvary itself. See in the crucifixion the flashing into light of an eternal fact, the nature of God's relation to sin, of the pain we inflict on his heart by our own wrongdoing. We are shown the world as the Father sees it, are called to live in harmony with his will and purposes, to hate the sins that make him mourn, to discover that the way of penitence lies open and direct to the Father's heart. Here you have the practical conditions of salvation, and in the active, free and holy love of God, ever seeking entrance, ever powerful if we but yield the gateway of our heart, is the substance of the Gospel.

John Wilhelm Rowntree, 1904
Faith and Practice (26.49)

ᚻere is the unfailing attraction of the life of Christ. It is a life which even to old age is always on the upgrade; there is always something calling for a joyful looking forward; it is a life where, across each revelation of God's grace as it comes to us is written, in letters of gold, Thou shalt see greater things than these. It gives full scope … to our desire for high adventure. No conceivable life can be so interesting, so stimulating, as that which we live in Christ.

William Littleboy, 1917
Faith and Practice (21.44)

The resurrection, however literally or otherwise we interpret it, demonstrates the power of God to bring life out of brokenness, not just to take the hurt out of brokenness but to add something to the world. It helps us to sense the usefulness, the possible meaning in our suffering, and to turn it into a gift. The resurrection affirms me with my pain and my anger at what has happened. It does not take away my pain, it still hurts. But I sense that I am being transfigured; I am being enabled to begin again to love confidently and to remake the spirit of my world.

S Jocelyn Burnell, 1989
Faith and Practice (26.56)

5. WORK CAN BE LOVE MADE VISIBLE

We can neither deny nor ignore the fact that our self-respect and our sense of being useful are closely bound up with the ability to hold down a job. Unemployment not only results in a lowering of living standards, it also induces a feeling of insecurity, of being unwanted, that we no longer have a place in the community. The fear of unemployment causes more unhappiness and does more to lower self-confidence than any other element in life... Thus any economic system which possesses an inbuilt tendency to reduce human involvement in its day-to-day engagements is both unnatural and unkind.

George Clarke, 1973
Faith and Practice (23.67)

Employers today, more and more, are demanding total commitment from their employees, often to the detriment of the employees' health and ability to participate in family and community life. People are facing decisions about giving all their energy to their company and having nothing left for themselves or anyone else. Some have the courage to opt for a more balanced approach to life and work, where paid employment has an important place, but also allowing sufficient leisure time to be an active parent, to enrich family and community relationships and replenish their own spiritual reserves.

Jane Stokes, 1992
Faith and Practice (23.56)

*A*rthur Basil Reynolds had that strong sense of the indwelling spirit of God which perforce claimed kinship with everything good and of enduring value in other men and in the world at large. He worked for the continuity of the good life and to preserve what was good from the past… He was a man of creative imagination, a craftsman who delighted in the work of his hands. He was a cabinet maker with the seeing eye and the unerring hand to translate his vision into actuality.

Hereford and Radnor
Monthly Meeting, 1961
Faith and Practice (23.58)

Unemployment is in truth an astonishing evil and calm acquiescence therein is discreditable. The stoic endurance of privation in times of shortage is noble, but poverty caused by enforced idleness, and in the presence of plenty, is so glaring an injustice that no man should accept it tamely.

Shipley N Brayshaw, 1933
Faith and Practice (23.69)

Voluntary work gives the sense of being able to give something – whether in time, money or expertise – and that is precious to the person doing the giving. The feeling of having contributed, the satisfaction of a job lovingly done, is the reward. We should not regard voluntary work as of less value because it is unpaid and the rewards intangible, nor should we exploit the goodwill of volunteers.

Jane Stokes, 1992
Faith and Practice (23.64)

For some it is right to give their whole lives explicitly to concrete forms of service, but for most their service will lie in the sheer quality of the soul displayed in ordinary occupations. Such ordinary occupations are sometimes an essential contribution to the liberation of another person for wider service and in any case, the inspiration of a dedicated life lived in simple surroundings, though often untraceable, may be profound in its reach.

Gerald Littleboy, 1945
Faith and Practice (23.66)

6. SILENCE CAN BE GOLDEN

Love silence, even in the mind. Much speaking, as much thinking, spends; and in many thoughts, as well as words, there is sin. True silence is the rest of the mind; and is to the spirit, what sleep is to the body, nourishment and refreshment.

William Penn, 1699
Faith and Practice (20.11)

So one approaches, by efforts which call for the deepest resources of one's being, to the condition of true silence; not just of sitting still, not just of not speaking, but of a wide awake, fully aware non-thinking. It is in this condition, found and held for a brief instant only, that I have experienced the existence of something other than 'myself'. The thinking me has vanished, and with it vanishes the sense of separation, of unique identity. One is not left naked and defenceless, as one is, for example, by the operations of the mind in self-analysis. One becomes instead aware, one is conscious of being a participant in the whole of existence, not limited to the body or the moment... It is in this condition that one understands the nature of the divine power, its essential identity with love, in the widest sense of that much misused word.

Geoffrey Hubbard, 1974
Faith and Practice (26.12)

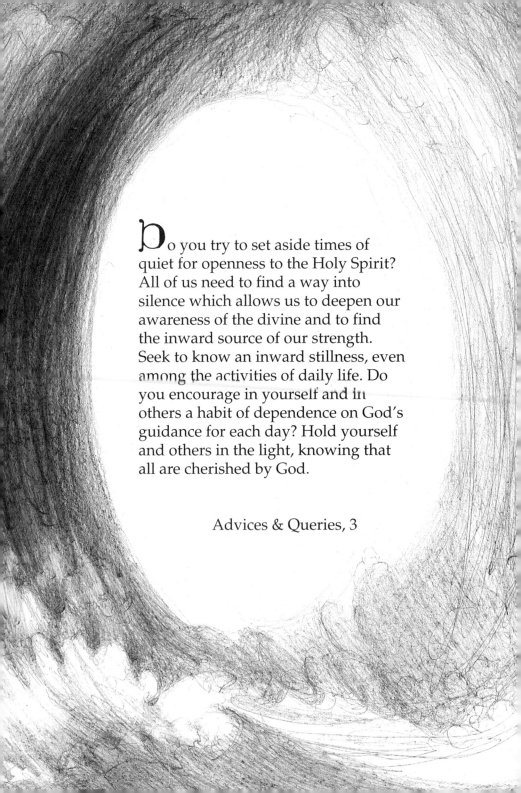

Do you try to set aside times of quiet for openness to the Holy Spirit? All of us need to find a way into silence which allows us to deepen our awareness of the divine and to find the inward source of our strength. Seek to know an inward stillness, even among the activities of daily life. Do you encourage in yourself and in others a habit of dependence on God's guidance for each day? Hold yourself and others in the light, knowing that all are cherished by God.

Advices & Queries, 3

*A*nd you, young convinced ones, be you entreated and exhorted to a diligent and chaste waiting upon God, in the way of his blessed manifestation and appearance of himself to you. Look not out but within. Remember it is a still voice that speaks to us in this day, and that it is not to be heard in the noises and hurries of the mind; but it is distinctly understood in a retired frame. Jesus loved and chose solitudes, often going to mountains, to gardens and seasides to avoid crowds and hurries; to show his disciples it was good to be solitary, and sit loose to the world.

William Penn, 1694
Faith and Practice (21.03)

The early Friends made the discovery that silence is one of the best preparations for communion with God and for the reception of inspiration and guidance. Silence itself, of course, has no magic. It may be just sheer emptiness, absence of words or noise or music. It may be an occasion for slumber, or it may be a dead form. But it may be an intensified pause, a vitalised hush, a creative quiet, an actual moment of mutual and reciprocal correspondence with God.

Rufus Jones, 1937
Faith and Practice (2.16)

I know of no other way, in these deeper depths, of trusting in the name of the Lord, and staying upon God, than sinking into silence and nothingness before Him. So long as the enemy can keep us reasoning he can buffet us to and fro; but into the true solemn silence of the soul before God he cannot follow us.

John Bellows, 1895
Faith and Practice (2.15)

7. LET'S TRY TO LIVE SIMPLY

Personal pride does not end with noble blood. It leads people to a fond value of their persons, especially if they have any pretence to shape or beauty. Some are so taken with themselves it would seem that nothing else deserves their attention. Their folly would diminish if they could spare but half the time to think of God that they spend in washing, perfuming, painting and dressing their bodies. In these things they are precise and very artificial and spare no cost. But what aggravates the evil is that the pride of one might comfortably supply the needs of ten. Gross impiety it is that a nation's pride should be maintained in the face of its poor.

William Penn, 1669
Faith and Practice (20.29)

If John Woolman's approach is the right one for the society of today it is not enough to go over our own behaviour in detail, cutting a bit here and pulling back a bit there; we must be concerned with our and society's attitude to life as a whole, to live answerable to the design of our creation.

Michael Lee, 1976
Faith and Practice (20.34)

$\mathcal{T}$ry to live simply. A simple lifestyle freely chosen is a source of strength. Do not be persuaded into buying what you do not need or cannot afford. Do you keep yourself informed about the effects your style of living is having on the global economy and environment?

Advices & Queries, 41

I want to list ten controlling principles for the outward expression of simplicity. They should not be viewed as laws but as one attempt to flesh out the meaning of simplicity into twentieth-century life. First, buy things for their usefulness rather than their status. Second, reject anything that is producing an addiction in you. Third, develop a habit of giving things away. De-accumulate. Fourth, refuse to be propagandised by the custodians of modern gadgetry. Fifth, learn to enjoy things without owning them. Sixth, develop a deeper appreciation for the creation. Seventh, look with a healthy scepticism at all 'buy now, pay later' schemes. Eighth, obey Jesus' injunction about plain, honest speech. Ninth, reject anything that will breed the oppression of others. Tenth, shun whatever would distract you from your main goal.

Richard J Foster, 1979
Faith and Practice (25.09)

8. WE SHALL STUDY WAR NO MORE

I told the Commonwealth Commissioners I lived in the virtue of that life and power that took away the occasion of all wars… I told them I was come into the covenant of peace which was before war and strife were.

George Fox, 1651
Faith and Practice (24.01)

The Society of Friends' Corporate Witness

All bloody principles and practices we do utterly deny, with all outward wars, and strife, and fightings with outward weapons, for any end, or under any pretence whatsoever, and this is our testimony to the whole world.

> A statement made to Charles II, 1660
> Faith and Practice (24.04)

When William Penn was convinced of the principles of Friends, and became a frequent attendant at their meetings, he did not immediately relinquish his gay apparel; it is even said that he wore a sword, as was then customary among men of rank and fashion. Being one day in company with George Fox he asked his advice concerning it. George Fox answered,

'I advise thee to wear it as long as thou canst.'

Not long after this they met again, when William had no sword and George said to him,

'William, where is thy sword?'

'Oh,' said he, 'I have taken thy advice. I wore it as long as I could.'

Samuel Janney, 1852
Faith and Practice (19.47)

The peace testimony is about deeds, not creeds; not a form of words but a way of living. It is the cumulative lived witness of generations of Quakers...

The peace testimony, today, is seen in what we do with our lives... We pray that we may work for a more just world. We need to train to wage peace.

London Yearly Meeting, 1993
Faith and Practice (24.11)

Gandhi was assassinated. Yet they did not fail.
Nor did they leave behind them the hatred,
devastation and bitterness that war, successful or
unsuccessful, does leave... This method of opposing
evil is one of which no nation need be ashamed, as
we should be ashamed of the inhumanities of war
that are perpetrated in our name and with our
support.

Kathleen Lonsdale, 1953
Faith and Practice (24.26)

national, racial and religious differences have not destroyed our common humanity but they have given it different faces which may tempt us to forget that all things that really matter, life and death, birth, love, joy and sorrow, poetry and prayer, are common to us all.

When our inward eye is opened we see humanity standing above all nations, more humble, more patient and far more enduring than all the kingdoms of this earth. This is the ultimate justification of our peace-making.

Duncan Wood, 1962
Faith and Practice (24.53)

We can learn to lay down carnal weapons, practising with weapons of the spirit: love, truth-saying, non-violence, the good news of God's birth and rebirth among us, imagination, vision and laughter.

Mary Lou Leavitt, 1987
Faith and Practice (24.55)

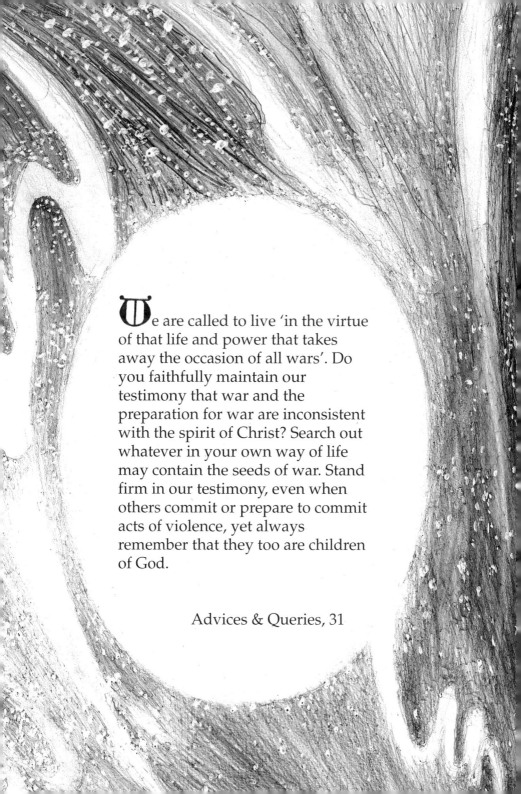

We are called to live 'in the virtue of that life and power that takes away the occasion of all wars'. Do you faithfully maintain our testimony that war and the preparation for war are inconsistent with the spirit of Christ? Search out whatever in your own way of life may contain the seeds of war. Stand firm in our testimony, even when others commit or prepare to commit acts of violence, yet always remember that they too are children of God.

Advices & Queries, 31

9. WE WILL LOVE BEAUTY AND REJOICE IN GOD'S CREATION

Along the path of the imagination the artist and mystic make contact. The revelations of God are not all of one kind. Always the search in art, as in religion, is for the rhythms of relationships, for the unity, the urge, the mystery, the wonder of life that is presented in great art and true religion.

Horace B Pointing, 1944
Faith and Practice (21.32)

We do not own the world and its riches are not ours to dispose of at will. Show a loving consideration for all creatures, and seek to maintain the beauty and variety of the world. Work to ensure that our increasing power over nature is used responsibly, with reverence for life.
Rejoice in the splendours of God's continuing creation.

Advices & Queries, 42

*A*ll of our senses are given to us to enjoy, and to praise God. The smell of the sea, of the blossoms borne on the wind, of the soft flesh of a little baby; the taste of a ripe plum or bread fresh from the oven, the feel of warm cat's fur, or the body of a lover – these are all forms of thanksgiving prayer. I am sure that it is as wrong to fail to delight in our bodies as it is to misuse them through excess. Not to be a glutton does not mean that we may not delight in good food; not to be ruled by lust does not mean that we must not enjoy the exquisite pleasure of sex; not to be slothful does not mean that we must never lie in the sun, not doing, just being. When Jesus said, 'I am come that they might have life, and that they might have it more abundantly' I do not think He was speaking of spiritual life – I think He meant us to have positive delight in all the good things in this wonderful world which his Father created.

Bella Bown, 1980
Faith and Practice (21.24)

This is a marvellous world, full of beauty and splendour; it is also an unrelenting and savage world, and we are not the only living things prone to dominate if given the chance. In our fumbling, chaotic way, we also make gardens, irrigate the desert, fly to the moon and compose symphonies. Some of us are trying to save species other than ourselves…

We have no reason to be either arrogant or complacent: one look at the stars or through a microscope is sufficient to quell such notions. But we have to accept our position in the world with as much grace, responsibility and fortitude as we can muster, and try to grow up to our mission of love in this tangle of prospects and torments.

Pamela Umbima, 1992
Faith and Practice (25.08)

There is a daily round for beauty as well as for goodness, a world of flowers and books and masterpieces… God is in all beauty, not only in the natural beauty of the earth and sky but in all fitness of language and rhythm, whether it describes a heavenly vision or a street fight, a Hamlet or a Falstaff, a philosophy or a joke: in all fitness of line and colour and shade, whether seen in the Sistine Madonna or a child's knitted frock; in all fitness of sound and beat and measure, whether the result be Bach's Passion music or a nursery jingle. The quantity of God, so to speak, varies in the different examples but His quality of fitness remains the same.

Caroline C Graveson, 1937
Faith and Practice (21.28)

A sudden concentration on a rainy August morning. Clusters of bright red berries, some wrinkled, some blemished, others perfect, hanging among green leaves. The experience could not have lasted more than a few seconds, but that was a moment out of time. I was caught up in what I saw: I became part of it; the berries, the leaves, the raindrops and I, were all of a piece. A moment of beauty and harmony and meaning. A moment of understanding.

Ralph Hetherington, 1975
Faith and Practice (21.27)

10. WE ARE ALL JOURNEYING TOGETHER

Some among us have a clear sense of what is right and wrong – for themselves personally if not for everyone else. They have a reassuring certitude and steadiness which can serve as a reference point by which others may navigate. There are others who live in a state of uncertainty, constantly re-thinking their responses to changing circumstances, trying to hold onto what seems fundamental but impelled to reinterpret, often unsure where lies the boundary between the fundamental and the interpretation…

Please be patient, those of you who have found a rock to stand on, with those of us who haven't and with those of us <u>who are not even looking for one</u>. We live on the wave's edge, where sea, sand and sky are all mixed up together: we are tossed head over heels in the surf, catching only occasional glimpses of any fixed horizon. Some of us stay there from choice because it is exciting and because it <u>feels like the right place to be</u>.

Philip Rack, 1979
Faith and Practice (20.06)

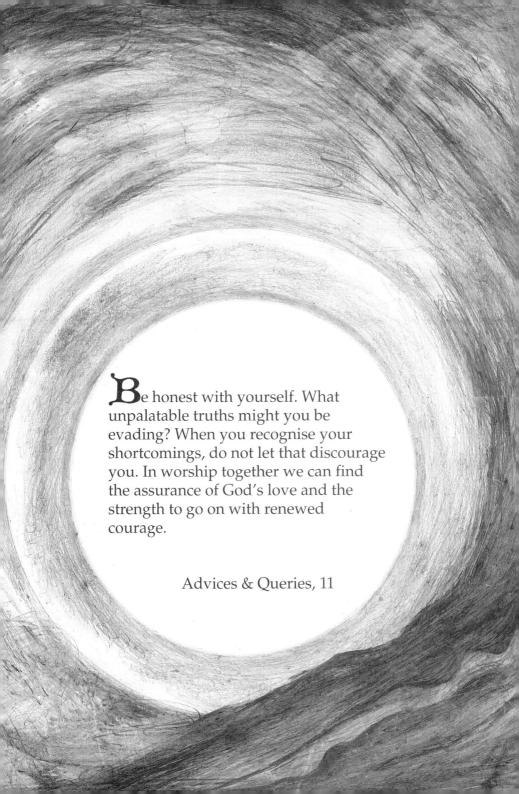

Be honest with yourself. What unpalatable truths might you be evading? When you recognise your shortcomings, do not let that discourage you. In worship together we can find the assurance of God's love and the strength to go on with renewed courage.

Advices & Queries, 11

It is because the learning process is continued throughout life that Friends are seekers as well as finders – not one or the other, but both. One only has to think of the need for a continual search for fresh language, unsoiled by use, to know that we must, if we care about truth, continue to be seekers. We may have a firm hold on old truth ourselves, but unless we are eager to find new ways of expressing it we may be unable to speak the word of life to others just when they most need it.

Ruth Fawell, 1987
Faith and Practice (26.18)

To you who are seekers, to you, young and old who have toiled all night and caught nothing, but who want to launch out into the deeps and let down your nets for a draught, I want to speak as simply, as tenderly, as clearly as I can. For God *can* be found. There *is* a last rock for your souls, a resting place of absolute peace and joy and power and radiance and security. There is a Divine Center into which your life can slip, a new and absolute orientation in God, a Center where you live with Him and out of which you see all of life through new and radiant vision, tinged with new sorrows and pangs, new joys unspeakable and full of glory... The reality of Presence has been very great at times recently. One knows at first hand what the old inquiry meant, 'Has Truth been advancing among you?'

Thomas R Kelly, 1941
Faith and Practice (26.72)

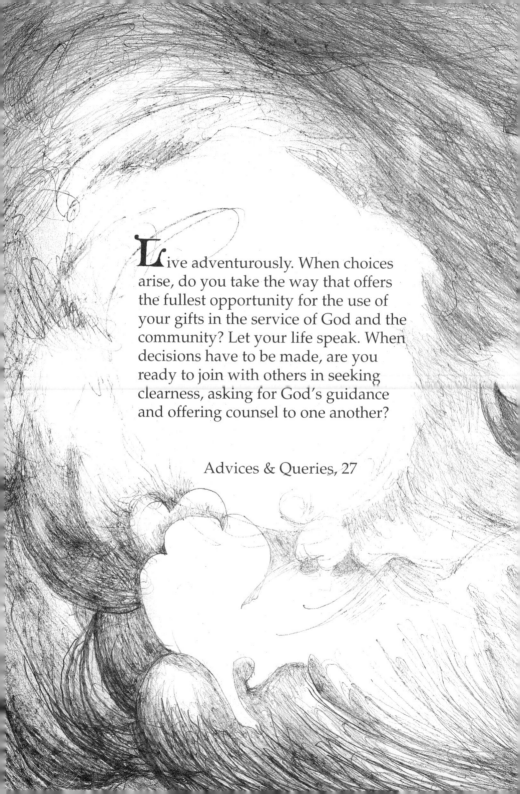

Live adventurously. When choices arise, do you take the way that offers the fullest opportunity for the use of your gifts in the service of God and the community? Let your life speak. When decisions have to be made, are you ready to join with others in seeking clearness, asking for God's guidance and offering counsel to one another?

Advices & Queries, 27

God is revealed to individuals through models suited to their temperaments and abilities; to communities through models suited to their culture. Nor will the interpretation of these models always be the same. Each one is only a guide to the truth that is greater than them all yet accessible in the nearest and simplest way...
As our experience widens we are brought closer to aspects of God which we did not understand before. But we are compelled to respect the experience and response of others. If there is no one model of the truth and if no model is essential then there is no basis for authoritarianism or heresy-hunts. Our own vision is widened by the vision of others.

Janet Scott, 1980
Faith and Practice (26.19)

*T*oday Science is rediscovering the creative mystery of the universe. The old self-assurance is largely gone. Within the first quarter of the twentieth century a revolution has taken place. The laws of mechanics no longer explain all things. The intellect of man has become aware of something strange and unpredictable at the very heart of existence. Matter and radiation have assumed a complexity which was hardly guessed at in the eighteen hundreds. The exploration of the minute structure of matter seems to take us as far into the unknown as does the exploration of the farthest reaches of space.

Howard C Brinton, 1931
Faith and Practice (21.42)

Perhaps the most neglected of all the advices is that we should live adventurously. If there is one wish I would pray the Spirit to put into our Christmas stockings, it is warmth, openness, passion, a bit of emotion that doesn't mind making a fool of itself occasionally.

Gerald Priestland, 1977
Faith and Practice (21.25)

True faith is not assurance, but the readiness to go forward experimentally, without assurance. It is a sensitivity to things not yet known. Quakerism should not claim to be a religion of certainty, but a religion of uncertainty; it is this which gives us our special affinity to the world of science. For what we apprehend of truth is limited and partial, and experience may set it all in a new light; if we too easily satisfy our urge for security by claiming that we have found certainty, we shall no longer be sensitive to new experiences of truth. For who seeks that which he has found? Who explores a territory which he claims already to know?

Charles Carter, 1971
Faith and Practice (26.39)

We know, with varying degrees of acceptance into awareness, our own weaknesses, and there is a tendency to think that others – who seem, on the surface, to be very sure and confident – do not struggle in the way we do. But many of those who appear to cope and be strong and tireless are indeed very different behind their masks. We are all wounded; we all feel inadequate and ashamed; we all struggle. But this is part of the human condition; it draws us together to find our connectedness.

June Ellis, 1986
Faith and Practice (21.14)

For a Quaker, religion is not an external activity concerning a special 'holy' part of the self. It is an openness to the here and now with the whole of the self... In short, to put it in traditional language, there is no part of ourselves and of our relationships where God is not present.

Harvey Gillman, 1988
Faith and Practice (20.20)

I am glad I was here. Now I am clear, I am fully clear. All is well; the Seed of God reigns over all and over death itself. And though I am weak in body, yet the power of God is over all, and the Seed reigns over all disorderly spirits.

George Fox, shortly before his death, 1691
Faith and Practice (21.49)

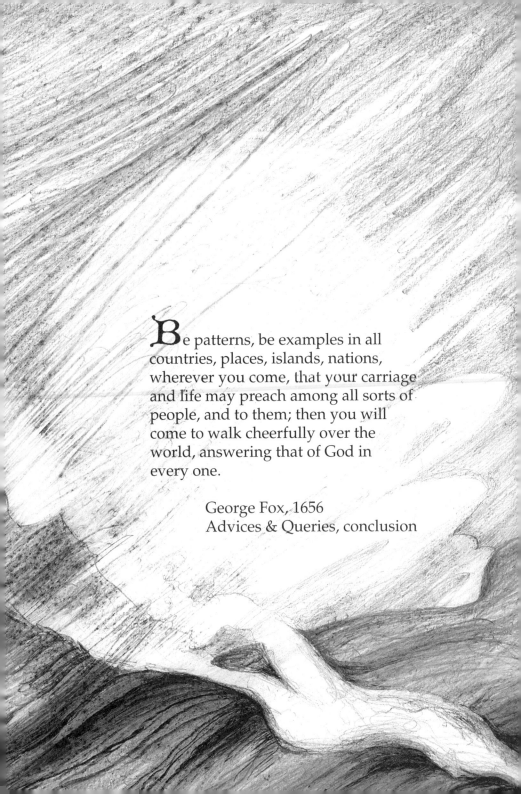

Be patterns, be examples in all countries, places, islands, nations, wherever you come, that your carriage and life may preach among all sorts of people, and to them; then you will come to walk cheerfully over the world, answering that of God in every one.

George Fox, 1656
Advices & Queries, conclusion

INDEX OF ADVICES & QUERIES

INDEX OF AUTHORS